# CHRISTMAS PROGRAMS for the Church

W9-CFZ-724

## Number 15

### Includes Thanksgiving material

Compiled by
Judith Ann Sparks

Cover by
Fred Sieb

STANDARD PUBLISHING
Cincinnati, Ohio                    8615

ISBN: 0-87239-514-6
© 1982. The STANDARD PUBLISHING COMPANY, Cincinnati, Ohio.
Division of STANDEX INTERNATIONAL CORPORATION.
Printed in U.S.A.

# Contents

## Thanksgiving
**Page**

The Thanksgiving Box ................. 5

Every Day Is a Day of Thanksgiving ..... 12

## Christmas

The Missed Blessing ................... 19

The Star ............................. 20

My Gifts ............................. 23

Let's Decorate the Wreath ............. 24

Christmas Joy ........................ 26

The Carolers ......................... 27

Centuries Have Passed ................ 31

Story Time ........................... 32

Bethlehem Evening News .............. 37

Jesus Loves the Little Children ........ 40

A Special Birthday Party .............. 43

Broke at Christmas ................... 56

Christmas Is More .................... 64

**Other available *Christmas* material:**

**8640**  Standard Christmas Program Book, Number 40
**8641**  Standard Christmas Program Book, Number 41
**8642**  Standard Christmas Program Book, Number 42
**8612**  Christmas Programs for the Church, Number 12
**8613**  Christmas Programs for the Church, Number 13
**8614**  Christmas Programs for the Church, Number 14
**3041**  Our Christmas Handbook

**Order direct from Standard or purchase at your local bookstore.**

# Thanksgiving

## The Thanksgiving Box

### by Mildred L. Wills

**Characters:**

Mary, Sue, Carol, Judy — Teen girls who are upset about contents of missionary box.

Jane Simmons, Beth Jordan, Lucy Kennedy — Ladies who are packing box.

### Scene 1

*(Mary, Sue, and Carol are seated in living room around a small table. Mary and Sue are looking at books. Carol is holding a paper and pencil.)*

**Mary:** It is hard to believe that next week is Thanksgiving already. Just a few days ago we were enjoying summer vacation.

**Sue:** Yes, time *does* fly. *(Sighs and lays book aside.)* Are you going away for Thanksgiving, Mary?

**Mary:** No, we're having Thanksgiving at home. We always look forward to the time together since Dad travels so much.

**Sue:** We always go to my grandmother's house for Thanksgiving. We love it! Grandmother and grandfather are *very* old-fashioned. We have a wonderful time, but— *(Voice trails off.)*

**Carol:** But what, Sue? Don't you enjoy old-fashioned things? I love them! My grandparents have a grandfather clock. It is a huge thing *(hand above head to indicate height)* and beautifully carved. I just love it! *(Leans forward eagerly.)* Some day I hope to have one of my own.

**Sue:** Oh, it isn't that I don't like old things. I *do!* But it's just that they think we should spend the entire day being thankful. Of course, we really *are* thankful, but—well, you know—I guess we just don't want to talk about it *too* much.

**Mary:** *(Leans forward.)* You know *(pauses)*—I think our grandparents have lived long enough to realize how many things we have to be thankful for. My grandmother sits in a wheelchair, but I never saw anyone find more things for which to be thankful on Thanksgiving Day than grandmother!

**Sue:** It doesn't sound as if she would have *anything* to be thankful for!

**Mary:** Oh, but she does! She keeps saying, "I'm so thankful that I can see and hear even if I cannot walk!"

**Sue:** Well, that really *is* being thankful! Where does she live?

**Mary:** She lives with my Aunt Beth Jordan.

**Carol:** It would be wonderful to feel that way about your misfortune! Of course, your Aunt Beth is a wonderful person, too. Always busy with church work. Right now she is helping mother and some other ladies pack a missionary box for the mountains.

**Mary:** Yes, but Aunt Beth isn't like grandmother. Grandmother is so unselfish. I'll bet Aunt Beth doesn't put anything in that box anyone would ever want!

*(Judy enters. Comes over to table and stands with hand on Carol's shoulder.)*

**Judy:** Hi, Chums! Why all the solemn faces?

**Carol:** We were just discussing Thanksgiving.

**Judy:** Well, I would never have guessed it to look at your faces.

**Mary:** We were really talking about Aunt Beth when you came in. Carol was saying how busy she always is with her church work.

Pull up a chair, Judy.

*(Judy moves chair to table and sits down.)*

**Judy:** I just came from the church. *(Cups chin in hands and looks dejected.)* They drove me out!

**Sue:** Drove you out! Why on earth did they do that?

**Judy:** Because I was making suggestions. You know they're packing a box to send to the mountains. And I think it's a shame the kind of stuff they're putting in it.

**Mary:** Stuff? What do you mean, Judy? Aunt Beth said it would make a real Thanksgiving gift. I understood that they were sending shoes and clothing and . . .

**Judy:** They are!

**Carol:** Well, what is wrong with that?

**Judy:** It isn't *what* they are sending—it is the *kind* they are sending! One of the ladies said, "I'll bet this will be the best Thanksgiving those poor people ever had!" And I said *(drawls),* "I wonder!"

**Sue:** Why, Judy, what do you mean?

**Judy:** Would you be thankful if someone sent you a lot of old, worn-out, unbecoming clothes? The things that they are packing are things that no one wants anymore. In fact, most of them are things that no one ever did want! They are just sending them to get them out of their way!

**Sue:** You really *are* upset, aren't you, Judy?

**Carol:** (*Rises quickly.*) I know what Judy means! We sing "Give of Your Best to the Master" every missionary Sunday, and then we send the very oldest and least attractive things we can find to the missionaries.

**Judy:** The thing that made me speak so bluntly was a purple satin dress with big red roses. And those awful high heeled shoes with just a strap across the toe. No one could possibly wear them on a smooth street, let alone on a mountain road.

**Mary:** Imagine wearing them on a hike up a mountain.

(*Girls all laugh—but Judy. Carol sits down.*)

**Judy:** You wouldn't think it was so funny if you could see the stuff. And the hats! I just wish you could see them. Those people need things that will be useful to them!

**Carol:** I think they really do mean well, Judy. If we could only make them think about it!

**Judy:** (*Jumps to her feet.*) That's what we will do. We will make them think!

**Sue:** What do you mean, Judy?

(*Girls all rise.*)

**Judy:** We planned to go on a hike this afternoon, re-member?

**Mary:** Of course, we remember, Judy. But what has that to do with the missionary box?

**Judy:** Meet at my house this afternoon and I will show you. Come on! We must get lunch before we can go.

(*All go out.*)

### Scene 2

(*Lucy Kennedy, Beth Jordan, and Jane Simmons are busily engaged in packing the missionary box. Items may be placed on the platform to give the appearance of a*

*Sunday-school classroom. Care should be taken to obtain as useless and gaudy items of clothing as possible. Old hats may be decorated to make their unsuitability more pronounced. Some shoes with very high heels and straps should be placed where they can be seen by the audience.)*

**Lucy:** I hurried back from lunch as fast as I could. I couldn't find some of the old clothes that I thought I had ready to bring. I had to leave the dishes for Judy. *(Busily she puts things in box.)* What have you there, Beth?

**Beth:** *(Holds up a ragged dress.)* Just an old dress that's been hanging around so long I got tired looking at it. It's too old to wear, but I hate to throw it away. And, you know, these old silk dresses don't even make good dust cloths.

**Jane:** I know just what you mean. Old dresses just hang around in the way. If it weren't for these missionary boxes, I don't know what we would do with this sort of thing. *(Holds up well-decorated hat. All laugh.)*

**Lucy:** I had several more pairs of old shoes that are completely out of style, but I searched everywhere and I couldn't find one pair.

**Jane:** Never mind! You'll find them after we get the box on its way.

**Lucy:** I don't think so. I searched everywhere for them. That's why I was so late getting back.

**Beth:** You know, I wonder if what Judy said this morning may be partly true. This does seem like a lot of junk!

**Jane:** Oh, I don't think so. Those poor people will be very thankful for these things. And the missionary can take out the things he needs first.

**Lucy:** I don't see how they could be choosy when we are *giving* the things to them. I agree with Jane. I think they will be very thankful over our box.

*(Mary, Sue, Carol, and Judy enter dressed in ridiculous, out-of-date clothes. Girls wobble and teeter on the heels of their shoes until the ladies look up in shocked surprise.)*

**Judy:** Did I hear someone say something about being thankful?

**Lucy:** Judy, what are you doing with those old clothes on? *(Turns to other women.)* Those are some of the things that I couldn't find.

**Sue:** We thought you wouldn't mind letting us wear them this afternoon. You were only going to put them in the missionary box anyway.

**Jane:** Of all the nonsense! Where do you intend to go in that silly outfit?

**Mary:** Why *you* know! Today is our hike to the mountain, and we wanted to go in real mountain hiking style.

*(Girls look serious, trying to keep from laughing.)*

**Beth:** Mary, you girls can't go hiking in those outfits. It would be impossible to get to the foot of the mountains in those awful high heels. You would probably break an ankle! You just cannot wear them.

**Judy:** But why not? Aren't you sending these things to the mountain people? If they can wear them, then they must be just the thing for our hike today.

**Beth:** Judy, you are right! You've made your point. We should all be ashamed.

**Jane:** Ashamed of what? Those people should be thankful—

**Beth:** *(Interrupts.)* Jane, it is no use. We all know that no one could use these things. Let's be honest.

**Jane:** I don't know what you mean. These things are sent in good faith to needy people. What more can we do?

**Beth:** We can send them something they can use! It's just that we haven't looked at it in the right way before. We are actually only giving away the things that we don't want and couldn't possibly use.

**Jane:** I still think—

**Beth:** We have just been following an old custom: "If you have something useless, send it to the missionaries."

**Lucy:** I'll confess I hadn't thought of it in that way until Judy spoke about it this morning.

**Sue:** We knew that you just hadn't thought about it. Then Judy told us what was being put in the box.

**Carol:** That's when we got to thinking about wearing the

things you were sending in the box. When Judy suggested that we try to show you how impractical they are, we thought up this stunt.

**Jane:** But what can we do? This is all that we have.

**Beth:** Not really, Jane. Not if we want to sacrifice. I have several pairs of comfortable shoes that I thought I might wear someday. The truth is, I probably never will.

**Lucy:** I have some dresses that I have been thinking the same thing about.

**Judy:** We would like to help if you'll let us. Mary has an uncle who owns a clothing store. He promised to give us some things later this afternoon. New things!

**Carol:** I have two pairs of shoes I would like to give, too. *(Grimaces.)* After wearing these *(points to feet)*, I really *am* thankful that I have other shoes.

**Sue:** I have several pairs of shoes that I am going to send because it is Thanksgiving time. I don't need so many shoes.

**Beth:** Good! *(Jumps up and starts unpacking box, stuffing the things into a paper bag.)* These things we will burn. I'm not sure they will even make a good fire.

**Carol:** On Sunday our Golden Text was: "Inasmuch as ye have done it unto one of the least of these my brethren, ye have done it unto me." Since many mountain people are Christ's own, we should give as unto Him.

**Beth:** We will start a new box tomorrow.

**Jane:** I think I see what you mean. Carol has made it very plain. I will see what I can find when I get home. I know I have some things that will be more suitable.

**Lucy:** Girls, go home and put those old clothes in the trash can, and tomorrow we will all meet here and start a new box. I am so thankful that we didn't send this box.

**Judy:** Now I guess we all have something for which to be thankful, and so will the missionary and his people in the mountains. Let's hope they get the box by Thanksgiving Day!

# Every Day Is a Day of Thanksgiving

## by Monica P. Malcolm

**Characters:**

| | |
|---|---|
| John | (Poor high-school student) |
| Joan | (John's classmate) |
| Tom | (John's classmate) |
| Kim | (John's classmate) |
| Mom | (John's mother) |
| Tony | (John's brother) |
| Mike | (John's brother) |
| Tina | (John's sister) |
| Jenny | (John's sister) |
| Maggie | (Elderly woman) |
| Narrator | |

*(The scenes are simple. In Scene 1 to indicate a school the characters carry books. John's books are shabby. In Scene 2 there is a table and six chairs. Real food can be used or the characters may pretend to eat. Scene 3 has a chair (preferably a rocker), a bench, and a table with a lamp or candle.)*

12

## Scene 1

**Narrator:** Our scene is a high-school campus the day before Thanksgiving recess. Joan, Tom, and Kim enter, talking about their plans for Thanksgiving. John walks behind them unnoticed. He is poorly dressed and his books are shabby. He hears the others talking and realizes that he has nothing wonderful to look forward to for Thanksgiving.

**Joan:** Boy am I glad there is no school tomorrow.

**Tom:** Yeah! I've had it up to here *(points with thumb to his neck)* with old Peabody's Math. If I have to bisect one more angle, I think I'll croak.

**Kim:** You think that's disgusting! I had to *disect* a frog! Yeah . . . spill the poor creature's guts . . . and just before lunch, too.

**Joan:** Look! Will you two forget about Math and Biology and listen to me for a moment? What are your plans for the Thanksgiving holiday?

**Tom:** *(Excitedly!)* Turkey . . . turkey . . . turkey!

**Kim:** Well, you know how it is at our house. We'll have enough turkey to have leftovers for the rest of the year . . . and perhaps New Year's, too.

**Tom:** Well, I could eat turkey for the whole year and not complain. When I think of that delicious bird roasted till it's brown and juicy . . . And all that stuffing falling over the side of the plate . . . Umm and the potato salad and the candied yams . . . And cranberry sauce and the gravy . . . Umm can't forget the gravy.

**Joan:** Tom, will you stop for Pete's sake. My mouth is watering so much you'd think a dam just broke.

**Kim:** OK. That's enough about Thanksgiving dinner. Let's plan a party for after Thanksgiving. We'll invite the whole class . . . except for you know who.

**Tom:** That's right! He's too shabby for my taste.

*(They exit. Enter John looking at test paper.)*

**John:** *(Talking to himself.)* B+? I know I should have scored an A on this paper. I studied so hard and I gave the right answers. Let's see . . . where did I go wrong? Peabody's remark says: "Need to pay more attention to neatness." OK. I'll work on that when we get back from the holiday.

Thanksgiving! What have I got to look forward to? For sure we won't have a turkey . . . Just the same old pork and beans. That's about the best we ever get. Ah, poor Mom. She does the best she can with the little she makes and all our hungry mouths to feed. I better hurry on home. She will be needing me to buy a few groceries before the store closes.
*(Exit.)*

## Scene 2

*(John's home. On stage is a table and six chairs. The table is set for dinner.)*
**Mom:** Dinner is served. Come and get it before it gets cold.
*(Four kids rush in.)*
**Mom:** Take it easy children. There's enough for everybody.
**Tina:** Mom, Jenny has the cup I like best.
**Jenny:** I got it first. Mom gave it to me.
**Mom:** *(To Tina.)* Alright, Sweetheart, don't start a fight. Here, you may have my cup. Where's John?
**John:** *(Shouting offstage.)* Coming, Mom. I'm just finishing this last sentence.
*(Enter John who sits down at the table.)*
**Mom:** Let's bow our heads, close our eyes, and give God thanks for what He has provided on this Thanksgiving Day. *(All bow heads and close eyes.)*

"Father, we thank You for putting food on our plates. We thank You for keeping our family together. For the job You've given me, and the love among us, we thank You, dear Lord. Amen."
*(They eat.)*

**Tony:** Mom, how come we never have a turkey?

**John:** Shut up and eat your beans, Tony!

**Mom:** Mr. Smith at the laundry promised to give me a raise. I promise you we'll have a turkey next Thanksgiving . . . No, we'll have a turkey for Christmas. I promise!

**Mike:** And stuffing, too?

**Tina:** And candied yams?

**Mom:** Yes, I promise.

**John:** Don't worry, Mom. It's OK. Oh, I almost forgot to tell you. The principal says he is impressed with my schoolwork. He says if I keep it up I may be eligible for a scholarship to medical school.

**Mom:** *(Enthused.)* That's wonderful, John. That's wonderful!

**John:** That's why I have been studying so hard. I know if I keep getting good grades I'll win that scholarship. You'll see! I'll be a doctor and I'll take care of you. You won't have to work in that crummy laundry anymore. *(Sadly.)* Excuse me, Mom, I'm going for a walk.

*(John exits.)*

### Scene 3

**Narrator:** John walks along the street, thinking out loud. He is very sad about what happened at the dinner table, and also he is remembering the remarks his classmates made about him.

**John:** I am too shabby for their taste. That was a mean thing to say about me. But why should that bother me? It's no worse than all the other things they've said before. Oh, I wish I could have been at their party this evening, but that's like crying for the moon. Why me? Why did I have to be born poor? That's where all my problems begin. If only I could have new clothes instead of these things from the Salvation Army thrift shop. If only I could buy new books instead of used ones. Then I would probably be accepted by the kids at school. Why me, Lord? Why me?

**Narrator:** As John passes an old house, he hears the beautiful words of a song. They catch his attention, and he pauses to listen.

> I'd rather have Jesus than silver or gold,
> I'd rather be His than have riches untold;
> I'd rather have Jesus than houses or lands,
> I'd rather be led by His nail-pierced hand
> Than to be the king of a vast domain
> Or be held in sin's dread sway;
> I'd rather have Jesus than anything
> This world affords today.

**Narrator:** John draws closer. He approaches the door of the old house and impulsively knocks.

**Maggie:** *(Feebly.)* Who is it?

**John:** I'm your neighbor. I live just down the road.

**Maggie:** The door is open. Come on in!

**John:** *(Enters.)* My . . . my name is John . . . John Martin. I . . . I . . . didn't mean to interrupt you, but I was passing by, and I heard the words of that beautiful song. I couldn't help myself. I just had to stop.

**Maggie:** That's alright, John. Ah, you can call me Maggie. Help yourself to a seat on that bench.

**John:** Thanks. May I stay for a little while?

**Maggie:** You surely may. I welcome your company. You know, the words of that song have become so very real to me. They soothe my soul so much. When I get to feeling lonely, I sing the songs from my old hymnal. Then it seems that I am not alone anymore.

**John:** But how can you sound so cheerful? I mean . . . it's Thanksgiving and here you are sitting all alone.

**Maggie:** But I'm not alone.

**John:** *(Looks around suspiciously.)* I don't see anyone here.

**Maggie:** Jesus is here. I know because He promises in His Word to be with me. I can feel His presence with me. Let me give you a little picture of what I mean. When the wind blows, do you see it?

**John:** No.

**Maggie:** But you can feel the breeze, can't you? And you

16

can see the movement of the leaves on the trees, can't you?

**John:** I surely can.

**Maggie:** Well, just like the wind, I cannot see Jesus, but I know He is near because His Word is here and gives me the comfort I need. He never leaves me, and that's the reason I sing like I do. But tell me, John, why are your eyes so sad?

**John:** Oh, nothing . . . I wouldn't want to bother you with my problems.

**Maggie:** What if I told you that I was expecting you?

**John:** *(Looks scared.)* I . . . I . . . don't know what you mean.

**Maggie:** Oh, don't be scared. I promise you I'm not a witch. I just felt that I would have a visitor today, and it turned out to be you. So whatever's bothering you, we can talk about it. We've got all evening.

**John:** Well, I was feeling a little down in the mouth because of Thanksgiving and all. Just for once I wished we could have had a real Thanksgiving with a turkey and all the extras. But we'll never be able to afford that luxury.

Then to add hurt to injury, my classmates are all having a party this evening. I'm not invited because, as they say, I'm too shabby for their taste. Maggie, it hurts so much to be treated that way.

**Maggie:** I understand how you feel, John. But if that's how they are, then they are not worth your company.

**John:** Maggie, you are incredible. Here I am feeling sorry for myself because I have so little, and here you are . . . you have even less. No family . . . no one to care for you . . . and yet you seem so happy. You have such comforting words to give.

**Maggie:** Christ is the source of my happiness. Because of Him every day is a day of Thanksgiving. I give Him thanks for the joy and peace and satisfaction that there is in my life, and for the hope I have in the next life.

**John:** Maggie, I would like to experience the happiness you have.

**Maggie:** You can! You can! Just remember there is always something for which you can be thankful. You've got life and strength and intelligence and a family. We could go on and on. You see, the more you thank God for what He has given you, the more He blesses you.

**John:** I never thought of it that way before. I guess I really do have a lot to be thankful for.

**Maggie:** Remember, John, whatever your situation, there is someone worse off than you are.

**John:** You know, Maggie, the principal at school told me that if I continue to keep my grades high I will be eligible for a scholarship to medical school.

**Maggie:** My, my, that's something! And you said you were feeling down in the mouth. That's something to throw your hands up in the air and shout about. God has given you the intelligence to be at the head of your class. You have the opportunity to become a doctor, raise yourself from a life of poverty, and help other people.

**John:** Maggie, you are so right. I do have a lot to be thankful for.

**Maggie:** Thanksgiving is not just having a turkey for dinner. Thanksgiving means thanking God for all He's done for us. Each day is a day of thanksgiving.

**John:** Thanks a million, Maggie. You've made me feel so much better. I have to go now, but I promise I will come to visit you again—as soon as possible. And I will bring my folks to meet you, too. Happy Thanksgiving, Maggie.

**Maggie:** Happy Thanksgiving, John.

*(John whistles on his way home.)*

18

# Christmas

## The Missed Blessing

Within the palace of Herod,
  The scribes did daily scan
The truths within the Scriptures
  Of God's eternal plan.

When Herod called the scribes one day
  To appear before his throne,
He asked of them, "Where is Christ born?"
  They immediately made it known.

"In Bethlehem of Judea's land,"
  Is what the scribes all said.
"It's written by the prophet, Sir.
  This many times we've read."

When the Wise-men were told of this,
  Their joy increased tenfold.
They continued on to find the babe
  In Bethlehem as foretold.

The scribes returned to work again
  As the Wise-men alone departed.
The scribes had missed God's greatest act
  Of seeing salvation started.

O foolish scribes with knowledge great,
  Yet your understanding's slow,
The child of which the Wise-men spake
  Is God dwelling here below.

Don't blame the scribes too harshly
  For we, too, have gone astray.
How many times do we forget
  Christ on His birthday?

# Exercises

## The Star

### by Carolyn Scheidies

*(Make large star; then cut off each point so it can be reassembled on a black background.)*

**Reader 1:** Reads Isaiah 52:7. Pauses and reads John 1:1.

*(Students 1 and 2 tack top star point to board. It is labeled WORD.)*

**Student 1:** Once God created man,
And a garden for his pleasure.
Satan came; man fell.
His fellowship with God was severed.

**Student 2:** But God did not let go—
His love for man was strong.
He promised to send a Savior—
His only begotten Son.

**Reader 2:** Reads Isaiah 7:14.

*(Students 3 and 4 tack up next star point. It is labeled PROMISE.)*

**Student 3:** Because of sin man had no peace—
Strife and war began.
Still God's promise brightly shone,
And His prophets told of the coming One.

*(Lights dim. Spotlight shines on prophet reading scroll.)*

**Student 4:** The coming One, the promised One,
Savior to all mankind,
The One who would bring love to earth
And peace to heart and mind.

**Reader 3:** Reads Isaiah 9:6.

*(Students 5 and 6 pin up star point labeled SALVATION. Students playing Mary and Joseph come in and sit down. Mary holds doll. While next students recite, spotlight moves from unfinished star to manger scene.)*

**Student 5:** Then at last it happened—
Early one dark Bethlehem morn,
As just a tiny little baby,
The promised King was born.

**Student 6:** A small little baby
Cradled in a manger,
Born as King of all,
But to the world a stranger.

**Reader 4:** Reads Luke 2:1-14.

*(Students 7 and 8 pin up star point labeled PEACE.)*

**Student 7:** The baby came to bring us peace.
Upon himself He took man's hate.
Then, as a man, the Son of God
Became man's sinful fate.

*(Spotlight on student holding cross.)*

**Student 8:** Nailed to a rustic cross
In agony He forgave my sin.
He made me His—
In love He died for me.

**Reader 5:** Reads John 1:1-5.

*(Students 9 and 10 pin up star point labeled LOVE.)*

**Student 9:** He brought us light and beauty
In a world of hate and pain.
Because He died upon that cross,
I'll never be the same.

*(Spotlight goes from manger scene to the cross.)*

**Student 10:**  From the manger to the cross,
            The beauty of His love shines round.
            That's why I want to tell you
            His precious love I've found.
**Reader 6:**   Reads John 3:16.

*(Students 11 and 12 pin up star center labeled CHRIST. Put spotlight on star.)*

**Student 11:**  There is war and pain and hate
            In our world today,
            God is dead and gone away
            You hear some people say.
**Student 12:**  But this is all that's missing,
            *(Points to star center.)*
            In the center of their lives.
            For the babe who came to Bethlehem
            Lives to make each one alive.
**Reader 7:**   Reads Matthew 2:1, 2 and John 5:24.

# My Gifts

## by Eleanor Pankow

(An exercise for eleven children)

1. The Wise-men came and offered gifts
   To Christ, the newborn King.

2. I wonder what will please Him now—
   What precious gift to bring?

3. I bring my tongue to tell God's love,
   A story old, yet new.

4. I bring my ears, that they may hear
   Kind things, and good, and true.

5. I bring my lips, that they may speak
   God's message far and near.

6. I bring my eyes, that they may see
   The lost who to God are so dear.

7. I bring my hands that they may do
   Good works for Him each day.

8. I bring my feet to walk earth's road
   In God's own holy way.

9. I bring to Him a gift of mine—
   My heart that's filled with love.

10. I bring to Him a promise
    To live for God above.

11. I bring to Him my very all—
    I'll answer "Yes" unto His call.

ALL: Yet any gift that we may bring,
      To lay at our Savior's feet,
      Cannot compare with His own gift—
      Salvation free and complete.

# Let's Decorate the Wreath

## by E. L. Russell

*(You will need to use seven youth—six younger and one older and taller to serve as the decorator. The six younger ones enter one at a time. They have foil-covered letters— red, blue, and silver. A large green wreath is hanging on the wall, out of reach of the six but just right for the decorator.)*

**Decorator:** Time is getting short and our Christmas program will begin soon. I wish I could do something to make this platform more attractive. That wreath is very nice, but it lacks something.

**1st Youth:** *(Enters and hands a red W to the decorator.)*
Worship the babe in the Christmas story,
Worship the Lord, the King of glory.

**Decorator:** Oh that is very nice. I'll hang the **W** up high on the wreath for it will look nice there.
*(Hangs W on wreath.)*

**2nd Youth:** Here is an **R** for Revealed.
Reported by angels, the Savior's birth
Revealed that God had come to earth.

**Decorator:** Thank you. That will look very nice on the wreath, too. *(Places it there.)* It would be nice to have a few more.

**3rd Youth:** **E** is for Eternal Life.
Eternal life abides within
When Jesus the Savior forgives sin.
*(Hands E to decorator.)*

**Decorator:** I don't know who thought of all this, but our wreath will be the finest one ever decorated. *(Places E on the wreath.)*

**4th Youth:** Assurance.
Faith will boldness bring,
And joyous carols we will sing.
*(Gives letter A to the decorator.)*

**Decorator:** We sure need assurance and that is what the Christmas message gives. It assures us of God's love. Let me place it on our wreath, too. *(Places A.)*

**5th Youth:** Trust in the Lord for He is Truth—
The Christmas message for age and youth.
*(Hands decorator a T.)*

**Decorator:** Trust and truth really go together. Thank you for this beautiful decoration. I'll put it up right now. *(Put T on wreath.)*

**6th Youth:** Holy the babe born that Christmas night—
He shared with all the holy light.
*(Hands an H to decorator.)*

**Decorator:** Now the wreath is ready to be seen! It has a message which is the very heart of Christmas. *(After placing the H on the green wreath, the decorator stands back and looks at it a moment. The other youth are still standing at one side, also admiring the results. They turn and face the audience.)*

**Youth:** If we will just decorate our lives with the great themes of the Bible, if we will just let Jesus be our Savior and Lord, what a beautiful witness we will be for Him.


Let's decorate our homes that faith in Jesus we will show.
Let's decorate our lives to glorify the Lord we know.
Let's all encircle Him and make a living wreath, a diadem—
No laurel crown would we on Him bestow.
So praise His name.
Exalt the Lord today.
Let's honor Him
And follow Him alway.

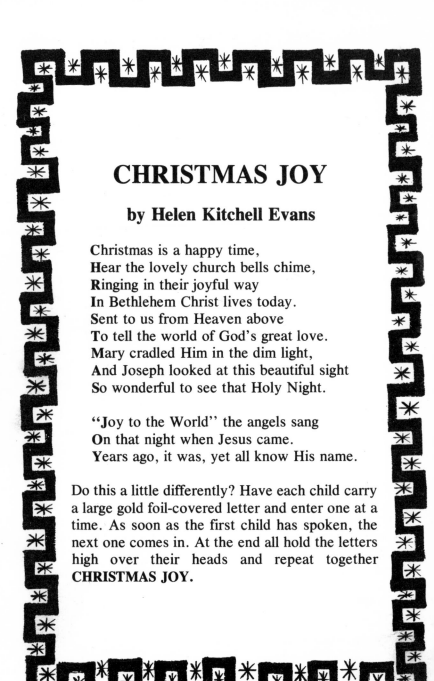

# CHRISTMAS JOY

## by Helen Kitchell Evans

Christmas is a happy time,
Hear the lovely church bells chime,
Ringing in their joyful way
In Bethlehem Christ lives today.
Sent to us from Heaven above
To tell the world of God's great love.
Mary cradled Him in the dim light,
And Joseph looked at this beautiful sight
So wonderful to see that Holy Night.

"Joy to the World" the angels sang
On that night when Jesus came.
Years ago, it was, yet all know His name.

Do this a little differently? Have each child carry
a large gold foil-covered letter and enter one at a
time. As soon as the first child has spoken, the
next one comes in. At the end all hold the letters
high over their heads and repeat together
**CHRISTMAS JOY.**

# THE CAROLERS

## by Marie M. Gattinger

**Characters:** Mr. Winters, an elderly man.
Mrs. Winters, an elderly woman.
Carolers, five—male and female.

**Time:** Present

**Setting:** Living room of the Winters' home. Mrs. Winters is seated near the table knitting. Mr. Winters enters from left. He picks up his glasses and a newspaper, sits down on a vacant chair, and begins to leaf through the paper.

**Costumes:** Mr. Winters: shirt, trousers, sweater, slippers.
Mrs. Winters: old-fashioned, mid-length dress, slippers, shawl.
Carolers: winter jackets, hats, scarves.

**Properties:** Two chairs, table covered with fancy cloth and Christmas cards, knitting, small table, newspaper, glasses, magazines, hymnbooks for carolers, plate of cookies.

**Lighting:** No special effects.

**Mr. Winters:** Only three days until Christmas!

**Mrs. Winters:** *(Continues to knit, but nods her head.)* Hmm.

**Mr. Winters:** Got all the shopping done?

**Mrs. Winters:** Hmm.

**Mr. Winters:** *(Puts down the newspaper.)* I haven't found where you've hid the Christmas cookies, yet. Sure hope you made lots of shortbread this year.

**Mrs. Winters:** I didn't do much baking this year; just a couple mincemeat pies. There'll be just the two of us here for Christmas. We'd be sick if we ate all that rich food.

**Mr. Winters:** I guess you're right. *(He gets up, picks up a magazine, and leafs through it.)* Did you get all the parcels wrapped and mailed?

**Mrs. Winters:** *(She makes an impatient wave of her hand.)* I did that days ago. The parcels to Mary's children had to be mailed extra early to be sure they'd arrive in England for Christmas. *(Sighs.)* It's getting to be such a big job now that we've grandchildren and great-grandchildren to buy presents for. There's all that shopping to do, and then all the gifts to be wrapped in tissue paper and again in heavy, mailing paper. *(She puts down her knitting and rearranges the Christmas cards on the table.)* And, of course, there's all the Christmas cards and letters to get ready.

**Mr. Winters:** *(He puts down his magazine and goes to look at the cards.)* We haven't seen Bill and Beth for years. It's sure nice to hear from old friends.

**Mrs. Winters:** *(She picks up her knitting again.)* Christmas is the only time we ever do hear from them. You'd think some of our old friends would write during the year, or come for a visit. I guess none of them really care what we're doing or what happens to us.

**Mr. Winters:** *(He sits down near his wife and picks up his paper.)* Now, Edith, you know they do care, but they all have their own families to visit.

**Mrs. Winters:** We have a family, too. But where are they? I'll tell you. They're scattered all over the world. Here we sit, two old people, shut in and alone at Christmas. Everyone else has family coming home for the holidays. Why, as soon as church is over on Christmas Day, off they go to celebrate. A lot anyone cares about you and me sitting here all by ourselves.

**Mr. Winters:** We'll manage. We'll manage. We can be thankful we still have each other. You know the children would be here if they could. They said they'd phone home on the 25th to wish us a Merry Christmas.

**Mrs. Winters:** Listen! I can hear music. *(She puts down her knitting, gets up, goes over to the window on the right,* *and looks out.)* It's the children from church. They're next door. *(She goes over to the table and makes quick, impatient tidying movements.)* They'll be here, next. *(Grumpily.)* I wonder how many wet tracks they'll leave on the floor this year? *(She pulls her shawl closer around her as she sits down on the left.)* They always let in so much cold air.

*(Offstage carolers sing first verse of "Hark! the Herald Angels Sing." There's a knock at the door. Mr. Winters answers it.)*

**Carolers:** *(All together as they crowd into the room.)* Merry Christmas! Merry Christmas!

**1st Caroler:** What's your favorite Christmas carol? We'd like to sing it for you.

**Mrs. Winters:** Oh, I don't know. It really doesn't matter. Sing whichever one you like.

**2nd Caroler:** Let's sing "Silent Night, Holy Night."

*(Carolers all sing.)*

**Mr. Winters:** *(Goes and sits down.)* That is my favorite carol. It was beautiful.

**3rd Caroler:** We'll be singing it at the Christmas Eve program in the church. You're both coming, aren't you?

**Mrs. Winters:** I don't think so. We won't get to church on Christmas morning, either. It's too far for us to walk through the deep snow.

**Mr. Winters:** I guess we'll just stay at home this Christmas.

**4th Caroler:** Don't you want to go to church?

**1st Caroler:** Won't you be lonely?

**Mr. Winters:** We'll manage. We'll manage.

**Mrs. Winters:** Our children are too far away to come home for Christmas, and we can't expect other people to think or care about us two old folks at such a time. Christmas is for families.

**5th Caroler:** But *we* care! That's why we came tonight.

**2nd Caroler:** We thought you'd like to have us come and sing for you.

**Mr. Winters:** (*Trying to smooth things over.*) We do. We do. It was beautiful.

**4th Caroler:** You're never really alone, you know. God is always with you, and He cares about you.

**3rd Caroler:** He cares about all of us. That's why on that first Christmas He sent a gift of love for the whole world.

**1st Caroler:** The baby born in Bethlehem was no ordinary baby. He was Jesus, God's Son, sent to earth.

**2nd Caroler:** Jesus is our friend—your friend. He's the kindest, dearest, and truest friend anyone can have. He loves you, and if you ask Him, He'll always help and comfort you.

**5th Caroler:** The play our Sunday-school class is putting on tells how Jesus was born to be our friend and Savior.

**4th Caroler:** I know my Dad would be glad to pick you up Christmas morning. Would you come?

**3rd Caroler:** My Mom said that she wished she knew of someone who'd like to come and help us eat all the food she's prepared. Would you come to my house for Christmas dinner?

**Mrs. Winters:** (*Dabs at her eyes with the corner of her shawl as she goes to the next room and brings in a plate of cookies which she passes around.*) We'd be glad to come to church and to your home. I didn't think anyone cared what happened to two old people like us.

**Mr. Winters:** I told you, Edith. People do care about us! (*Turning to carolers.*) Thank you for coming tonight. It's meant so much to us.

**Mrs. Winters:** I'm really looking forward to Christmas, after all.

(*Carolers turn to leave.*)

**5th Caroler:** Good night! We'll see you at church.

(Carolers leave singing first verse of "Joy to the World.")

# Twenty Centuries Have Passed

## by Rega Kramer McCarty

Twenty centuries after Christ,
The town of Bethlehem
Remains as it was long ago,
A place to honor Him.

A place of worship more renowned—
The birthplace of our Lord,
Where still the holy truth abides
In the beauty of His Word.

Still shepherds watch their flocks at night,
Upon Judean hills,
And still the people shape their lives,
According to God's will.

Candles light the sacred scene,
And voices lift in prayer.
The spirit of the Christ child
Seems ever present there.

Twenty centuries have passed,
Yet much remains the same—
Pilgrims come to Bethlehem
To worship in Christ's name.

# Story Time

## by Elvera Wilken

*(Set stage to look like a living room—artificial hearth, chair, pictures, plate of small cookies, etc. Place an easel where an available flannelboard may be used.)*

**Welcome:** We are glad you have come today—
Hope you will join us at the hearth
Of my Sunday-school teacher who will tell
The ever-new story of Jesus' birth.

*(Teacher takes her place on stage and sets up easel. Several children knock at door.)*

**Teacher:** I am so glad you have come to hear our story today. It is the story of the birthday of Jesus. We are going to tell it in pictures on the flannelboard. Won't you please sit down on the floor? *(Motions to them to sit.)*

*(Singing is heard in the distance. Then another group comes to the door singing carols. Possibly two or three could be sung.)*

**Teacher:** Thank you for your songs. You are just in time to hear our Christmas story. Won't you please join us? *(Motions for them to come in. They also find places on the floor. Teacher puts flannelboard on easel, puts on hills, trees, rocks, sky, etc. She may sit or stand as she tells the story.)*
Out on the hills of Judea,
Shepherds were watching their sheep.
The night was dark and quiet—
The whole world was asleep.
*(Place shepherds on board.)*
Then out of the eastern sky
Shone a light bright as day.
It startled the lolling shepherds

As on the hillside they lay.
*(Place star and bright rays on board.)*
The chill of the evening shadows
Was lurking all around,
Until the light from Heaven
Warmed the cold Judean ground.
*(Soft music is played in background.)*
The shepherds heard celestial music
By heavenly angels sweet.
There on a Judean hillside
Heaven and earth did meet.
The shepherds were frightened
At the unusual light.
Never before had they seen
Such a marvelous, yet awesome sight.
Then the voice of an angel,
Above the celestial tones,
*(Place angel on board.)*
Brought words of comfort
As the light upon them shone.
"Fear not: for, behold, I bring you good tidings of great joy, which shall be to all people. For unto you is born this day in the city of David a Saviour, which is Christ the Lord. And this shall be a sign unto you; Ye shall find the babe wrapped in swaddling clothes, lying in a manger."
*(Remove angel from board.)*
A multitude of angels sang,
Over and over again,
*(Place angels on board.)*
"Glory to God in the highest,
And on earth peace, good will toward men."
The angels departed from sight,
*(Remove angels from board.)*
But the stars remained.
*(Put stars on board.)*
Let us go and find this baby
Just as the angels proclaimed.

They quickly began their journey,
Guided by the bright starlight.
*(Remove resting shepherds and place walking shepherds on board.)*
They would not have known the way,
But they trusted the angels were right.
So they went to David's town—
Led by starlight so bright.
To a lowly little stable
In the town they were led.
*(Place stable on board.)*
Inside they found the manger,
Just as the angel had said.
*(Place manger on board.)*
In the manger lay the baby Jesus,
And Mary and Joseph were there, too.
*(Place figures on board.)*
The shepherds bowed and worshiped
The angel's message was true.
Three eastern kings on camels came,
To worship the newborn babe.
Costly gifts they brought,
Which before the Christ child were laid.
*(Place Wise-men on board.)*
Still today we read and tell the story—
Again and again it is told—
Of the marvelous birth of our Savior.
A story that never grows old.

Now wasn't that a good story? Do you have any questions?

*(Children ask questions and the teacher gives the answers.)*

1. Where was Judea? *(Today it is a part of the nation of Israel. Then it was an ancient region in the southern part of Palestine.)*
2. What were shepherds? *(Shepherds were very hum-*

ble men who spent their time caring for flocks of sheep—during the day on the mountainside and at night in an enclosure.)

3. Where was the star? (*It shone in the eastern sky but moved and guided the Wise-men to the baby Jesus.*)
4. What is celestial music? (*Heavenly music, coming from the sky.*)
5. How many angels were there? (*Our story doesn't tell, but the Bible speaks of a multitude, hosts, or throngs.*)
6. What does that mean? (*Many—a large number.*)
7. What is good tidings? (*Good news. This good news was that Jesus our Savior was born.*)
8. What is David's town? (*Bethlehem. The Bible foretold that our Savior would be born in the hometown of David.*)
9. Why was He born in a stable? (*People came from miles around to be taxed because of a demand made by the king. The crowds were so large that there weren't any rooms left in the inns. The stable was the only place that was available.*)
10. What is an inn? (*Today we would say hotel or motel. It was a place where travelers could stay to rest and sleep.*)
11. Is this Jesus our Savior, too? (*Oh, yes! He came into the world for everyone—all colors, all nationalities, you and me.*)
12. How can we help? (*You can love all people, do good deeds, obey your parents, work hard, be kind and courteous, and tell others about Jesus being their Savior.*)

(*Teacher then takes a tray of small cookies from the table and passes them. As the children take the cookies, they thank her casually and leave.*)

### For Smaller Children
(*Children enter carrying a very small table, cloth, cake,*

*and a very large candle. The teacher lights the candle after it has been put on the cake.)*

**Speaker:** A birthday cake for Jesus
We bring today.
We remember His birthday
In this very special way.

**Children
Sing:** Happy birthday to You,
Happy birthday to You,
Happy birthday, dear Jesus,
Happy birthday to You.

We love You today,
We love You today,
We love You, dear Jesus,
We love You always.

**Speaker:** Each day should be a Christmas Day—
Not just the one in December—
Reminding us how and why Jesus came.
May we daily strive to remember.

Because God loved, He gave His Son.
Now we give gifts to friends.
Let us give gifts that really last—
On which life and eternity depend.

*(At this time four smaller children bring gifts, wrapped and labeled accordingly. Coming from the right, they speak and place their gifts near the cake or under a tree.)*

**1st Child:** I bring joy *(place gift; point to audience)* to you.
**2nd Child:** I bring love *(place gift; point)* to you.
**3rd Child:** I bring peace *(place gift; point)* to you.
**4th Child:** I bring goodwill *(place gift; point)* to you.

**Song:** "Joy to the World."

# Bethlehem Evening News

## by Jean Koenig

**Props:** Large cardboard box with a working door. Paint "The Inn" on one side. It hides the manger scene from the audience until the proper time. A desk is needed for the Anchorman and microphones are needed for all reporters. By spotlighting the different areas of the stage, the other scenes can be set up according to the facilties available. *(Fill blank spaces with names.)*

**Anchorman:** Good evening, this is _____ with your evening news. The decree from Caesar Augustus concerning taxes has resulted in crowded conditions in our city tonight. We also have reports of a disturbance on the hills outside of town. We'll switch you now to _____ who is on the scene in Bethlehem.

**1st Reporter:** Here we are on location outside the city of Bethlehem, where a disturbance has been reported. I see some shepherds approaching. Excuse me! Could you tell me what has happened here tonight?

**Song:** ''Angels We Have Heard on High.''

**1st Reporter:** This has been _____ reporting from the hills outside of Bethlehem.

**Anchorman:** We will now switch you to our correspondent in the Far East.

**1st Correspondent:** Good evening. I'm _____. We have reports tonight that several kings have been getting ready for a long journey, taking precious gifts with them. We find this situation unusual and are waiting for an interview. Pardon me, but could you tell us what your plans are?

**Song:** ''We Three Kings of Orient.''

**1st Correspondent:** This has been _____ reporting from the Far East.

**Anchorman:** Now we will switch to our reporter in Jerusalem, to see if there is any word from official sources concerning the unconfirmed rumors of a new king.

**2nd Reporter:** This is _____ on the scene in Jerusalem. Although we have been standing outside the palace yard, we have been unable to interview anyone close to the king. So I asked a group of people on the streets of Jerusalem for an interview. Perhaps they can give us their views concerning the rumor that a new king has been born in Bethlehem. If this is true, what would you say?

**Song:** ''Joy to the World.''

**2nd Reporter:** This has been _____ reporting from Jerusalem.

**Anchorman:** We will now go back to our reporter who is still on the scene in Bethlehem.

**1st Reporter:** The shepherds whom we interviewed earlier

are now on the streets of Bethlehem, excitedly talking to everyone they meet. Excuse me, but could you tell us what has happened since our last interview?

**Song:** "Go Tell It on the Mountain."

**1st Reporter:** This has been ＿＿＿＿ reporting from Bethlehem.

**Anchorman:** Another of our correspondents is located near one of the crowded inns in Bethlehem waiting to interview the innkeeper.

**2nd Correspondent:** Good evening. We are still searching for firm evidence of the birth of a new king. *(Knocks on door.)*

**Innkeeper:** No room! No room!

**2nd Correspondent:** I'm not looking for a room. I'm a reporter and would like to know if you have rented a suite of rooms to a party of royal heritage today.

**Innkeeper:** A suite of rooms! Why, we are so crowded I had to send a pregnant woman to the stable to have her baby! And you ask about a suite of rooms! *(Slams door.)*

**2nd Correspondent:** This has been ＿＿＿＿ in downtown Bethlehem.

**Song:** "What Child Is This?"

**Anchorman:** We have finally located the center of activity, and our reporter is on the scene outside a stable in Bethlehem.

**1st Reporter:** As we have followed this story concerning a new king, we have been led ultimately to this humble stable. According to all our information, it houses this mystery king. We will try to gain admittance to the stable. *(Steps forward.)*

**Two Women:** *(Leaving the stable.)* Shshshshshsh!

*( All lights go out. Inn is removed. Spotlight is put on the manger scene.)*

**Song:** "Silent Night, Holy Night." *(Can be hummed while Luke 2:10, 11 is read. Then a group in the background can sing the last few words of the carol—"Christ, the Savior, is born, Christ, the Savior, is born.")*

# Jesus Loves the Little Children

## by Betty Harmon

**Introduction:** Christmas Day belongs to all,
    Not just black or white or brown,
But whosoever will believe—
    For these God sent Christ down.

From every nation children come
    To share in Christmas joy.
We'll learn of various customs
    From each girl and from each boy.

**Norway** *(carries sheaf of wheat on long pole):*
    When Jesus was born in a manger,
        The animals round Him stood.
    The sheep, the cow, the donkey, the dove
        Saw Christ so kind and good.

In my country which is Norway,
    We, too, would be kind and good.
Because Christ loved the birds and beasts,
    At Christmas we feed extra food.

We put out special fodder
    For the cattle in our herds,
And we tie wheat atop tall poles—
    A Christmas dinner for the birds.

**England** *(carries small log):*
    I am from merry England,
        And I celebrate Christ's birth
    With a flaming, crackling Yule log—
        With caroling and with mirth.

On Christmas Eve in my home,
    Before the Yule log is lit,

Each member of my family
Upon the log, in turn, will sit.

According to our traditions,
This custom will bring good cheer,
And the Yule log will burn brightly
Until the coming of the New Year.

**Germany** *(carries small Christmas tree):*
Tannenbaum—the Christmas tree—
Came from my country—Germany.

We decorate it with real candles aflame
And light them on Christmas Eve night.
When we see it ablaze, we remember anew
Christ Jesus who is the true light.

**Italy** *(carries colorful flowers):*
We have no firs or evergreens
In my country of Italy.
So with many flowers we prepare
For Christ's nativity.

Our shepherds sing in every town,
Especially at carpenter shops,
Recalling Christ, the workman,
Whose work still never stops.

**Czechoslovakia** *(carries nativity scene and wear crowns):*
Czechoslovakia is the land
From which we three have come.
We have many Christmas customs,
But we will tell you about just one.

Two friends and I go caroling—
We carry the Bethlehem scenes—
On our heads we wear golden crowns,
Impersonating the three eastern kings.

They came bearing gifts for the Christ child,
  And we, too, our offerings would bring,
For now, as well as in those days,
  Wise men worship the great King.

**France** *(carries holly or songsheets):*
  In France we gather holly,
    And sing our glad noels.
  "Noel" means "happy birthday"—
    Our joy at Christ's birth it tells.

  The first noel, the Bible says,
    Was sung by an angel choir.
  The shepherds heard it and believed,
    While watching sheep by evening fires.

**Mexico** *(carries paper lantern):*
  If you lived in my country of Mexico,
    You might celebrate in this way:
  Take part in a *posada processional*
    The night before Christmas Day.

  We dress as Joseph and Mary,
    And knock on our neighbor's door.
  We ask them for a night's lodging,
    As Joseph did long before.

  At first, as did the innkeeper,
    He will rudely refuse us a room.
  But when he hears I am Joseph with Mary,
    He opens his heart and his home.

**Postlude:**    Let not our hearts be busy inns
      That have no room for Thee.
    But cradles for the living Christ
      And His nativity.

JAMES E. SEWARD

# A Special Birthday Party

## by Margene Pride

**Characters:**      Mother Taylor              Grandma Taylor
                             Father Taylor               Grandpa Taylor
                             Billy Taylor                   Mrs. Davis
                             Katie Taylor                  Mrs. Garvey
                             Roger Taylor                 Mr. Janson
                                              Jesus

**Costumes:** Jesus *(Biblical dress),* other cast members wear comfortable, informal clothes—not too dressy *(remember they don't know about the surprise guest).*
**Time:** One week before Christmas—everyone is busy with plans and activities.
**Place:** Living room of the Taylor family.

## Scene 1

*(Mother is at a table busily wrapping gifts for Christmas. Katie enters.)*

**Katie:** Mom, will you have time to help me hem my dress for the Christmas party? I've got so much to do—work, choir practice, shopping . . .

**Mother:** Now, Katie, you know I told you to start early on that dress—so you would have it finished in plenty of time. I just don't know when I can find the time, but I'll try. Put it on the sewing machine with the other mending.

**Katie:** *(Katie leaves with dress.)* Thanks, Mom. You're a doll.

**Mother:** A doll? You can certainly tell Christmas is just around the corner. I'll never get everything done in time.

*(Billy, smiling and in a pleasant mood, enters the room from another way. He is carrying a manger scene.)*

**Billy:** Hi, Mom, is Roger home yet? *(Pauses and looks around room.)* I got the manger scene out. Where do you want me to set it up?

**Mother:** No, your brother isn't home yet. He had a basketball practice after school. *(Pauses, thinking.)* Set the manger scene on the mantle. That would be a good place.

**Billy:** Oh, *(disappointed)* I was hoping Roger could play some basketball with me. *(Pauses.)* Mom, would you help me . . . ?

**Mother:** *(Before Billy can finish speaking.)* Billy, stop right there. I absolutely cannot take on any more jobs. Whatever it is, you'll have to do it yourself.

**Billy:** But, I only wanted you to . . .

**Mother:** *(Interrupts.)* Sorry, I've got too many things to do before we can celebrate Christmas around here.

*(Billy places manger scene on mantle, then dejectedly goes over and sits down on couch. He starts looking at a book or magazine. Mother continues wrapping gifts. Father enters*

44

*carrying a cup of coffee and humming a carol. He sits down in a chair or on couch.)*

**Mother:** *(Looks up as father enters. Looks glum and is not very enthusiastic.)* You're in a good mood.

**Father:** *(Cheerfully.)* I like this time of year. Everybody seems much more cheerful—present company excluded. Why so glum?

**Mother:** Oh, so much to do and not enough time to do it in.

**Father:** You know it's the same every year, and we always manage to get done.

**Mother:** Yes, I guess we do, but I wish everything wasn't so hectic. *(Pauses, thinking.)* You know, when you think about it, the first Christmas was an upsetting time, too—for a lot of people. Especially for Mary and Joseph. They traveled so far to get to Bethlehem to enroll for paying their taxes. Then trying to find a room—and Mary giving birth to Jesus in a stable. How have we all gotten so far away from the real reason we celebrate Christmas—Jesus' birthday?

**Father:** *(As father is talking, mother finishes wrapping.)* We all let the hustle and bustle of Christmas get the best of us at times. But when we look at our manger scene, or hear some of the carols that are sung, it makes us remember. Here, let me help you with those packages.

**Mother:** *(Father goes over and picks up wrapped packages. Mother speaks, then they exit.)* I suppose so, but for so many people Jesus is just a baby in a manger. They seem to forget He grew to manhood and sacrificed His life for us.

**Billy:** *(Waits until mother and father exit, then begins talking disgustedly to himself.)* I don't know why everybody gets so upset. All they talk about is shopping, wrapping gifts, dresses, and parties. Rush here; rush there! It *is* going to be Jesus' birthday—that's what we're supposed to be celebrating. *(More excited.)* Boy! Wouldn't it be neat to have a birthday party for Jesus and have Him come in person. Wonder who would come? It could be a surprise party. Only the ones com-

ing would get the *surprise*. I bet Mrs. Davis and Mr.
Hanson would come. And the "kids" from church.
And Grandma and Grandpa. (*By this time Billy is in a
reclining position on the couch. He yawns and settles
down onto a pillow.*) Yeah! A birthday party for a
"special friend"—that's what I'd tell them.
(*Dim lights all the way down or pull curtain.*)


## Scene 2

(*Same setting. Billy is putting up a "Happy Birthday,
Jesus" banner. Mother, father, Roger, and Katie enter.
They carry items for a table, put presents under the tree,
and straighten books on the table.*)

**Billy:** I hope everybody comes for the party. Hey, Roger,
help me put this banner up. (*Roger goes to help Billy.*)

**Father:** Just how many people did you invite, Billy?

**Billy:** Oh, all my friends! I can hardly wait. They're going to
be so surprised when they see Him.

**Mother:** See Him?

**Billy:** Jesus, of course. The party is for Him.

(*Roger and Billy are still working on the banner. At Billy's
statement they all express surprise and begin to ad-lib with
various expressions such as "What did he say?" "Jesus,"
and "Who?"*)

**Roger:** Boy! Leave it to Billy. His imagination is running
wild again. *Where* do you get your ideas? I thought this
party was for your friend Mike. (*Pauses.*) You *surely*
don't expect Jesus to show up, do you?

**Billy:** I didn't say the party was for Mike. I said my "*special
friend*," and I *just know* He will be here. I asked Him
especially to come.

(*Mother, father, Katie, and Roger look at each other be-
wildered, shrug, or make other appropriate motions. Door-
bell rings.*)

**Katie:** I'll get it. (*Answers door.*) Put your coats in the
closet.

46

*(People come in with various items Billy has told them to bring. They are all talking, greeting each other, and finding seats. Teen choir enters with cast and sits together on the floor in one area. Younger departments can already be seated on front rows. Billy exits out another way while everyone is coming in. Mrs. Davis and Mr. Hanson are standing talking to Billy's parents. When everyone gets in and settled, Mrs. Davis speaks.)*

**Mrs. Davis:** *(Looks around room.)* Where's Billy? And who is this "special friend?"

**Father:** He was here just a minute ago. *(Looks around, calls.)* Billy! Billy! Your guests are all here.

**Mrs. Davis:** Billy is such a nice young man. Always wanting to help me with something. I just couldn't refuse his invitation.

**Mr. Hanson:** Me either. He was so secretive about whom the party was for. A "special friend" he said.

*(As Mr. Hanson finishes speaking, Billy enters from offstage with Jesus. He takes Him to a special chair marked with ribbon or "Guest of Honor" sign. All start talking to each other, looking toward Jesus. Various expressions of surprise can be ad-libbed at this time from the cast and teen choir. Mr. Hanson and Mrs. Davis sit down during this time. All during the party Billy stays right by Jesus' side, sitting on the arm of His chair or standing by Him.)*

**Billy:** This is my "special friend" I wanted you to meet. The party is for His birthday.

**Mother:** *(Very flustered.)* But, Billy, I never dreamed—We could have helped you more with plans—*(Voice trails off.)*

**Billy:** Mom, you've been so busy getting things ready for Christmas. And, remember, you said I'd have to do it myself.

**Mother:** Yes, I did, didn't I? If we had only known *Jesus* was coming! *(Mother earnestly fusses around table then is seated in the background as Jesus speaks.)*

**Jesus:** I'm sure what Billy has planned will be just fine. I haven't had a special birthday party in a long time. I do remember one special birthday when I was a boy. After that one, I was allowed to go to the temple with my earthly father, Joseph. Of course, my mother, Mary, told me many times about the events of my birth in Bethlehem.

**Billy:** I always like to hear about when I was born. How excited Dad got and everything. I like to hear the story of when You were born, too. I asked Grandpa to bring his Bible and read about it for us.

**Grandpa:** *(Remains seated but leans forward in seat—very flustered.)* Now, Billy—*(Hesitates.)* I'm sure Jesus would rather we talked—or something. Son, I just wish you had prepared us more for your "special friend."

**Billy:** But, Grandpa, you knew Jesus is my friend. We're always talking about it.

**Grandpa:** Yes, I know *(hesitantly),* but I was expecting someone else. *(Looks at Jesus.)* Billy asked me to do this for Your birthday gift. He said You didn't need anything and he thought You would like it.

**Jesus:** Mr. Taylor, I've heard you read the Word many times. I think Billy made a wise request. It always pleases Me and My Father when the Bible is studied and read.

**Billy:** Grandpa, you make it sound so real. If I close my eyes, I can almost see everything that happened when you read.

**Grandpa:** All right. I'm going to read Luke's account of what happened. *(Grandpa then reads Luke 2:1-20.)*

**Jesus:** Thank you, Mr. Taylor. To bring this message to others in such a way that they can visualize the occasion is truly a special talent. You give Me a gift each time you do it.

*(Billy leans closer to Jesus.)*

**Mother:** Billy, please don't crowd Jesus so. Let some of the others have a chance to see.

**Jesus:** Mrs. Taylor, you bring to mind a time when My disciples rebuked those bringing children to Me. Again

I say, "Suffer little children, and forbid them not, to come unto me; for of such is the kingdom of heaven" (Matthew 19:14).

**Mother:** I'm sorry, I just thought—

**Billy:** That's OK, Mom, Jesus understands. *(Turning to Jesus.)* I asked my Grandma to bring the cake. She's a super cake maker. *(Billy turns and speaks to Grandma.)* Show it to Him, Grandma.

**Grandma:** Jesus isn't interested in my baking cakes, Billy. He has so many other concerns to attend to. *(Pauses.)* But if I'd only known the cake was for Him, I could have made something more appropriate—and it's so small. *(Looks around at all the guests.)* And there's so many people here. *(Grandma picks up cake from table and shows it to Jesus. Cake is in the shape of a sheep. A member of the congregation who is good at baking could provide the cake.)*

**Jesus:** *(Looks at cake.)* It's a very nice cake, and I'm sure it will taste good. You have helped so many people when they have been sick or bereaved by using your cooking talent. Remember, I was hungry and you gave Me something to eat, I was thirsty and you gave Me something to drink, I was a stranger and you invited Me in . . . Truly I say to you, to the extent that you did it to one of these brothers of Mine, even the least of them,

49

you did it to Me (Matthew 25:35, 40). I'm sure Billy had a reason to request you make a cake that looks like a sheep.

*(Grandma puts cake back on table and helps mother or speaks to her. Then she returns to her seat as Billy speaks.)*

**Billy:** Sure. You're the good shepherd. That's what Grandpa always says. And You know, when Grandpa was reading I could almost hear singing, like the angels sang. I know You must like music. We sing about You in church all the time. Katie sings *real* good. She's going to sing You a song for your birthday. *(Looks toward Katie.)* Come on, Katie.

*(Katie is seated with her friends on the floor. She stands nervously.)*

**Katie:** *(Horrified.)* Bill—eee! Why didn't you tell me I was singing for Jesus. You *surely* don't expect me to sing now.

**Billy:** Sure I do. Jesus would like that, wouldn't You? *(Looks at Jesus.)*

**Jesus:** That would be very nice.

**Katie:** But—but—I haven't practiced enough and—and— *(Acts speechless.)* I don't know what song to sing.

**Billy:** You sing for Jesus all the time at church. Sing the song you've been practicing for the program tomorrow. *(Several people speak out encouragement to Katie.)*

*(Reluctantly Katie goes over and stands near the piano.)*

**Katie:** Well, all right, but this doesn't seem like much of a gift for Jesus.

**Jesus:** The joy you give others by using your voice to talk and sing about Me is a very precious gift.

**Katie:** *(Sings. Several comment on the beautiful song, especially Grandma.)* Thank you, Grandma. *(Looking at Jesus.)* And Jesus, I'll remember every time I sing what you said about using my voice.

**Billy:** *(Looking at Roger.)* Roger, why don't you and your friends sing some more songs. I really like the little drummer boy song. I like to pretend to be him. I think Jesus will like it, too.

50

**Jesus:** *(Smiles and nods.)* Yes, I would like that.

*(Teen choir sings. Depending on the stage, they can remain seated or stand as they sing two songs. When the choir finishes singing everyone claps.)*

**Billy:** Wasn't that pretty, Jesus? *(Jesus nods.)* Are you having a good time at your party? *(Billy should sound enthusiastic.)*

**Jesus:** Yes, Billy, I'm having a very nice time.

**Billy:** I asked Mrs. Davis to write one of her poems about Christmas. She's going to read it now. You know, she sends me the nicest cards when I'm sick, and on my birthday, too.

**Jesus:** Yes, I've noticed that she remembers so many people at special times. I know how much they all appreciate it. Also it pleases Me when people are so thoughtful and loving.

**Mrs. Davis:** *(Nervously, hesitantly. Remains seated, but leans forward in her chair.)* Lord, *(reverently)* I didn't realize I would be reading this poem to You, but after Billy asked me to write a poem about Christmas I just sat down and wrote how I felt about it.

**Jesus:** I know the poems you write come from your heart. My Father in Heaven has given so many ways for people to express themselves to others. Yours is a special talent. Please read it for us.

**Mrs. Davis:** *(Reads an original poem by member of congregation if possible.)*

**Billy:** Thanks, Mrs. Davis. I hope some day I can write poems like that.

**Jesus:** Even if you can't write poems, Billy, whatever you do, do it for Me.

**Billy:** Some of the other "kids" from church have been practicing for their part in the program, and just now they're going to do it for You.

*(Younger departments sing at this time. Everyone claps after each group sings.)*

**Jesus:** This has been such a wonderful party. I'm enjoying every minute of it.

**Billy:** Do you really like it? Do you like all the gifts the people have brought? Oh, I hope so. I wanted this to be a special party *just* for You.

*(Jesus nods and smiles. Puts His hand on Billy's shoulder then speaks.)*

**Jesus:** You know, Billy, you may already have found your special talent. You have made lots of friends, and you invited them all here to meet Me.

**Billy:** They *already* knew who You were. I wanted them to know You better—like I do. And I *just knew* You would come.

**Jesus:** *(Repeats Matthew 18:3, 4.)* "Verily I say unto you, Except ye be converted, and become as little children, ye shall not enter into the kingdom of heaven. Whosoever therefore shall humble himself as this little child, the same is greatest in the kingdom of heaven. And whoso shall receive one such little child in my name receiveth me."

**Mr. Hanson:** *(Stands and approaches Jesus.)* Billy was so insistent that we all come. Since we all think so much of him, we didn't want to disappoint him by not coming to the party. He asked me to bring some of my blueprints to show You. He said You would be interested since You had helped Your father in his carpenter shop. I understand now why he said that. *(Unrolls blueprints and points out several things.)*

*(Mr. Hanson will stay by Jesus and Billy for next few lines.)*

**Billy:** Mr. Hanson has some of the neatest tools, and you should see some of the things he's made.

**Jesus:** I have seen them, Billy. *(Jesus looks up from prints at Billy.)*

**Billy:** Oh! That's right. I forgot.

**Jesus:** I've also noticed how Mr. Hanson has time for inquisitive little boys, and how he patiently explains to them how to make things and how to use certain tools.

*(Jesus hands blueprints back to Mr. Hanson who returns to his seat.)*

**Billy:** Yeah! Mr. Hanson is one of my *very* best friends. We talk about lots and lots of stuff. He's my Sunday-school teacher, too, and he's told me all the stories about You.

**Jesus:** Yes, I know. *(Looks around at guests.)* I see many teachers here. I hope someday that you will be telling other boys the stories about Me—like Mr. Hanson does you.

**Billy:** Oh, I'm going to. *(Pauses and looks around for Mrs. Garvey.)* Mrs. Garvey, come on and show Jesus your gift.

**Mrs. Garvey:** *(Very fluttery and flustered.)* It's really not very much—uh, oh, dear, my hair is a sight. I should have worn my other dress. Dear me, Billy, you *really* should have told me about your "special friend."

**Billy:** You look just fine, Mrs. Garvey. Jesus likes you just the way you are. Go ahead! Show Him.

**Mrs. Garvey:** Well, if you insist. *(Hands some pictures to Jesus.)*

**Jesus:** *(Looking at pictures with Billy.)* I see what you mean, Billy. Mrs. Garvey does paint pretty pictures.

*(Mrs. Garvey stands by nervously tugging dress, twisting handkerchief, etc.)*

**Billy:** And that's not all. In the summer she has the most flowers in her garden. She's always giving them away to sick people, and she brings them to church for Sunday mornings, too.

**Mrs. Garvey:** Goodness, Billy, Jesus doesn't want to hear all that. I'm just sharing with others the beautiful flowers God gives me. It's such a joy to make other people happy.

**Jesus:** Billy, you certainly do have many nice friends. Their gifts to Me mean so much. Giving of themselves is more precious than any gift they could buy.

*(As Jesus speaks, Mrs. Garvey returns to her seat. Roger stands up and comes closer.)*

**Roger:** Bill, old pal, you've sure pulled a good one this time. I thought your imagination was running wild again when you told us earlier Jesus was coming. *(Hesi-*

*tates*.*)* I'm really not very prepared with a gift for Jesus. *(Very embarrassed, Roger holds out an unwrapped model car box.)* I bought a model for Mike, thinking it was his party. Guess I'm going to have to listen to you more closely next time you tell me something.

**Billy:** That's OK, Roger. *(Turns toward Jesus.)* He helps me and Mike make the neatest models. And sometimes he and his friends let us play ball games with them. We have so much fun. For an older brother, he's pretty nice, even if he does tease me a lot.

*(Roger could either lightly punch Billy on the arm or mess up his hair. He remains standing near Billy until Jesus finishes speaking, then he sits down.)*

**Jesus:** You know, Billy, I'm sure Roger doesn't realize how much you look up to him and his friends. I've seen how he takes time for you in many different ways. *(Looks at Roger.)* Roger, it pleases me to see young people your age take time for these younger ones. Your example to them has more impact on their lives than you know. As for the model, go ahead and give it to Mike, and help him with it. That will be your gift to Me.

*(Father rises from seat and goes and stands by mother. They come in a little closer to Jesus.)*

**Father:** Son, your mother and I didn't know. You didn't tell us what gift to bring. We don't have a gift for Jesus.

**Billy:** Sure you do. Your gift is letting me have the party here. Where else could I have had it?

**Jesus:** Billy's right, Mr. Taylor. You and your wife are always opening your home to others. Your gift of hospitality is appreciated, but the best gift from you are your children, Billy, Katie, and Roger. By bringing them up in a Christian home, teaching them to love Me—you are giving them to Me.

**Mother:** We didn't realize what Billy was saying when he wanted to have a party for a "special friend." We thought maybe five or six of his schoolmates were coming. *(Looks around.)* So many people. I didn't think he knew so many people. What a change in their lives he has made by inviting them here.

**Jesus:** Yes, people in Isaiah's time didn't understand a lot of what he was saying either. He was trying to tell them of My coming to earth. One verse comes to mind that could very well apply to Billy. "The wolf also shall dwell with the lamb, and the leopard shall lie down with the kid; and the calf and the young lion and the fatling together; *and a little child shall lead them*" (Isaiah 11:6).

**Father:** Billy has certainly led us to realize that too many times at Christmas we think of just the baby in the manger. He has made *You* a very real part of his life. A *"special friend"* he has complete faith in.

**Jesus:** Mr. Taylor, I hope you do appreciate what an unusual boy you have. *(Turning to Billy.)* Thank you so much for having the party for Me.

**Billy:** I'm *so* glad you came. I'll remember this night *forever and ever.* Mr. Hanson always tells me You're with me all the time, even if I can't see You, but this has been *super.*

**Grandpa:** *(Leans forward in his chair.)* Before everybody has to leave, let's all sing one last song.

**Billy:** OK, Grandpa. You pick it out.

**Grandpa:** All right—"Silent Night, Holy Night" is a favorite of mine. Come on, everyone, let's all sing. *(Motions for the audience to sing, too. Everyone sings one verse. As they are singing, the lights dim all the way down or the curtain is pulled. Everybody but Billy exits. All party items must be removed—banner, cake, etc. Assign members of cast to do this. Lights come back on, or the curtain is pulled open. Billy is asleep on the couch. Mother comes in, pats his shoulder, and wakes him.)*

**Mother:** Billy! Billy! Wake up! It's suppertime.

**Billy:** Boy! What a neat party it would be. *(Excitedly.)* Mom, wait until you hear my dream.

*(Lights dim. Mother and Billy exit.)*

# Broke at Christmas

## by Carl L. Fisher

**Characters:** Michael Gregory *(father)*
Betty Gregory *(mother)*
Tim Gregory *(child)*
Sue Gregory *(child)*
Pete Gregory *(child)*
Linda Gregory *(child)*
Jerry Gregory *(child)*
Brother Tom *(minister of local church)*
Rodney O'Brien *(bill collector)*
Jack *(borrower)*
Bill Brown *(friend repaying favor)*

**Props:** Living room of Gregory home. Have enough furniture to make setting look good.

## Scene 1

*(Scene opens with Michael and Betty in living room. He is sitting on couch making hand puppets. Betty is sitting in rocking chair knitting.)*

**Michael:** Betty, I just don't know what to do. I don't have enough money to get presents for the children. Do you think they will like these puppets? *(Holds one out for Betty to see.)*

**Betty:** Sure they will. They love anything that you make for them.

**Michael:** Well, I'm worried. *(Gets up and paces the floor.)*

**Betty:** Mike, I know you've done the best you can. They will understand. Don't worry—just enjoy the Christmas season. You know what they say, " 'Tis the season to be jolly."

**Michael:** Yeah! I'd be jolly if everyone would pay me what they owe me. Why I'd have plenty of money then!

*(Oldest son Tim enters the room eating an apple, just in time to hear the last few words.)*

**Tim:** *(Shows his muscles.)* Hey, Dad, want me to collect for you?

**Michael:** No, Son, I gave the groceries and loaned the money to them in good faith. If they never pay, I'll not hold it against them. *(Shrugs shoulders.)*

**Tim:** I guess so. *(Leaves room eating his apple.)*

**Michael:** Oh, Betty, I just remembered I have some fruit and candy left over at the store. I can put that in their stockings as a little something extra. *(Seems to feel better as he begins to move about the room.)*

**Betty:** *(Smiles.)* Somehow I just feel like everything will be all right.

*(After a short pause there's a knock at the door. Betty answers it.)*

**Betty:** Why it's the preacher! Come on in, Brother Tom. It's been a while since you been over here. *(She moves pillows from the couch.)* Here, sit and make yourself comfortable.

**Tom:** *(Sits down.)* Well, I hope you folks are enjoying Christmas. It's my favorite time of the year.

**Betty:** *(Gasps.)* Oh, Brother Tom—we've got money problems and Mike is worrying himself sick over it.

**Michael:** Yes, but we shouldn't burden him with our problems. He's got enough of his own. Besides—

**Tom:** *(Interrupts.)* Look, I've always got time to hear troubles, and I help when I can. Besides, it's my job and it's a pleasure to be of service to anyone in the church congregation.

**Betty:** Well, Mike gave out so much credit and loaned so much money that it looks like we may lose the store and everything else we own.

**Tom:** Have you talked to God about it? You know what the Word says. "You reap what you sow." God will see to it that in His own time and His own way the money and credit you have given to others will come back to you. He keeps His promises.

*(About that time their other four children come hustling through the front door.)*

**Sue:** Hey, Mom, guess what? We got parts in the Christmas play at school.

**Pete:** It's about Jesus being the greatest gift to us.

**Linda:** Yes, and I got the part of Mary!

**Jerry:** And I'm one of the Wise-men!

**Sue:** Mom, I think it's just wonderful to think about what Jesus did. He was born to die—as a ransom for my sins. *(Breaks into tears.)* Oh, Mom! I'm glad I know the real meaning of Christmas.

**Betty:** Yes, I am, too, Susan. *(Gives her a hug.)*

**Linda:** Well, we've got to practice. See you later.

**Michael:** Fine, but aren't you going to say "hello" to Brother Tom?

**Sue:** Oh—Hi, Brother Tom. We're sorry. We didn't mean to be rude.

**Tom:** That's all right. I wish more people would get that excited about talking about Jesus.

*(Children leave the room.)*

**Betty:** Brother Tom, could we fix you something to eat or drink?

**Tom:** No, thanks, I really have to go. But before I do I would like to have a word of prayer.

**Michael:** That would be fine—go ahead.

**Tom:** Heavenly Father, we come before You this day on behalf of the Gregory family. Father, You know their financial circumstance. Because of their kindheartedness, they are now in a difficult financial situation—they are in need. We know You own the cattle on a thousand hills—and the hills they roam on. We know that You take care of Your own. Lord, we pray just now that Your blessing will be on this family, and in Your own way that You will help them through this trying time. In Jesus' name we pray. Amen.

*(Brother Tom leaves.)*

**Michael:** If we had more people like him, the world would be a much better place.

**Betty:** That's right, Honey.

## Scene 2

*(Scene opens with Michael and Betty in living room listening to carolers outside.)*

**Betty:** Mike, listen to those carolers—doesn't that put you in the Christmas spirit?

**Michael:** It certainly does. I'm beginning to feel much better. There is nothing like Christmas carols being sung to lift a person's spirits.

*(Knock at the door. Mike answers it.)*

**Rodney:** Hello, Mr. Gregory?

**Michael:** Yes—

**Rodney:** I'm Rodney O'Brien from the loan company. I thought on my way home I'd stop by and see if you're going to be able to take care of your account. It is overdue and since I OK'd the loan myself, I felt that I should check with you.

**Michael:** But I called your office and told them I couldn't pay right now. Didn't they tell you? I just can't pay it right now.

**Rodney:** We're not going to be able to wait very long. We'll have to take your furniture and other things that you used as your collateral.

**Betty:** But it's Christmas! Can't you wait a little longer?

**Rodney:** I know it's Christmas, and I'm sorry, but we're in business. We can't keep on waiting on our overdue accounts. I'll be back after Christmas is over, and we'll have to have our money then.

*(He leaves. Michael turns to Betty.)*

**Michael:** Some *friendly* loan company!

**Betty:** Well—it could be worse.

**Michael:** I don't know how. If only the people who owe me would repay. We'd be in great shape. We could pay off the loan, reopen the store—*(He lets his voice trail off.)*

**Betty:** Oh, Mike, it sounds good, but don't get your hopes too high.

**Michael:** Remember yesterday when Brother Tom was here? I can't explain it, but while he was praying I just knew that God would take care of things. I don't know how, but I do know that whatever happens it will be His way of taking care of our problems. I have had such a contented feeling ever since I realized that God is in control.

*(There's a knock at the door. Michael opens it.)*

**Michael:** Well, hello Jack. We haven't seen you for a long time. Come on in and tell us how things have been going with you.

*(Jack comes stomping in like he owns the place. Makes himself at home. Sits down and props his feet on a table or stool.)*

**Jack:** Hey, Betty, got any coffee and cake in the kitchen? *(Turns to Michael.)* You know she makes the best cakes in town.

**Betty:** *(Reluctantly.)* Well, I'll see. *(Leaves the room.)*

**Jack:** Say, Mike, while she's in the kitchen there's some-

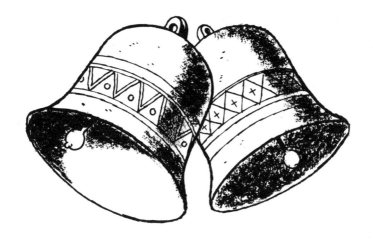

thing I'd like to talk over with you—a little business deal.

**Michael:** Oh, no! I remember your last business deal. You said if I loaned you $2,000 you could strike oil on your land, and you'd pay me back in just a few weeks. The closest thing to oil that you found was muddy water, and the closest thing to my $2,000 I've seen is you. So my answer is, "Not this time!" I've already lost a fortune listening to you. Not again.

**Jack:** Oh, but it's different now. All I need is about $3,000 to buy a new drill.

**Michael:** As ridiculous as I think it is, if I had the money I would probably try to help you. But to be perfectly frank, I simply do not have the money.

**Jack:** Well, I'll be going. No need digging in a dry well.

*(Michael walks to the door with him.)*

**Michael:** You know if I had it, it would be yours.

*(Michael closes the door and sits on the couch. He begins to read the paper. Betty enters the room with a tray of coffee and cake.)*

**Betty:** Well, where's Jack?

**Michael:** When he found out I was broke, he left.

**Betty:** It was probably good riddance. Do you want some coffee and cake?

**Michael:** No thanks. I don't feel much like eating right now.

*(Betty takes the tray and leaves the room.)*


## Scene 3

*(The family is gathered in the living room singing "Silent Night, Holy Night." After the song is over, they begin to open their presents.)*

**Michael:** OK, Linda, here's yours. Sue—Pete, these are for you. And Jerry here's yours. Last but not least this is yours, Tim. *(Hands out gifts.)*

**Jerry:** Dad, did you give Mom hers yet?

**Michael:** Not yet, Jerry. Here it is, Betty. *(Hands her a gift.)*

**Betty:** And this is for you. *(Hands gift to Michael.)*

**Michael:** OK. Everyone open up.

*(Ribbon and paper fly as children open gifts. Mother and dad wait.)*

**Children:** Oh boy! Just what I wanted. Thanks, Mom! Dad! How did you know?

**Michael:** *(Looks at Betty.)* Go ahead! Open yours!

**Betty:** *(Opens her present. Inside is a coat. Holds it up.)* It's just beautiful, but how did you get the money?

**Michael:** Oh, I did a little work on the side for Mr. Wilson, and what he paid me was just about enough.

**Betty:** Thanks, Honey. Now it's your turn.

**Michael:** *(Open his gift and finds a guitar. He gasps.)* How did you ever afford this?

**Betty:** Well, I did a little laundry and a little ironing. The children collected pop bottles. Putting our money together, we were able to get you something that we knew you really wanted.

**Michael:** You know, this has been the poorest Christmas we've ever had, but I really do believe that it has been our best.

*(Later in the day, Betty and Michael are alone. Someone knocks at the door.)*

**Michael:** I wonder whom that could be? *(Answers the door.)* Well, it's Bill Brown. Come on in out of the cold.

**Bill:** Listen, I can't stay long, but I did want to see you before I catch my plane. I was able to make a quick trip home for Christmas and little else.

Remember a couple of years ago when I came to you for a loan? I said you were my last hope. I'd been everywhere else and all of them had turned me down.

**Michael:** Yeah, but—

**Bill:** Well, I've made good because of you. I bought the farm in Kansas I told you about. A few months back oil was found on it, and since your money bought that land, I've always thought that a piece of it was yours. The oil profit for your piece of the land is $24,000. *(Counts out the money.)*

**Michael:** *(Sits down on couch.)* I don't know what to say.

**Bill:** Just don't say anything. Enjoy your Christmas. I didn't write or call you before, because I thought what a nice present this would make at Christmastime.

Well, I'll see you the next time I'm in town. Right now I have a plane to catch. Merry Christmas!

*(Bill exits.)*

**Betty:** Oh, Honey, he doesn't know how merry our Christmas has become. I never dreamed that anything like this could happen.

**Michael:** Me either! Now we can reopen the store and pay off our bills. It will be such a relief to be able to call the loan company and tell them I have the money to pay that overdue loan. But best of all, won't it be wonderful to see the look on Brother Tom's face when we tell him. Our tithe on this money will help so much with the expansion program at church.

**Betty:** Yes, it will be wonderful, and it's even more wonderful to know that in some way we reap what we sow.

# CHRISTMAS IS MORE

## by Enola V. Feldman

There were no bells
To ring the joy
Of Jesus' holy birth,
But loving angels
Sang when He
Became a child of earth!

Instead of rope
Of tinseled gold
Looped round a Christmas tree,
A loving star
Lit desert paths
That Orient men might see!

Though not a sweet
Was there that night—
(Like candied treats we give)—
Our loving God
Sent His sweet Son
To show us how to live!

So, greater than
The tinkling bell,
The twining tinsel rope,
Is Christmas joy
That came that night
With messages of hope!

A hope for all
Who crown Christ king—
And Him alone they prize.
Christmas is more
Than just a holiday.
It's our passport to Paradise!